바라보는 대상이 된다는 것은
To be the object of gaze is to be

옮긴이_안인숙 In Suk Ahn

영어영문, 영어번역, 영어교육 전공
2018년 시사문단에 시로 등단
제14회 빈여백동인 문학상 수상
시집 『그녀가 피아노 치는 이유』 『그냥 쉼』 『흐르는 봄』 『뒷모습을 보려 노력합니다』
옮긴 책으로는 그녀의 시집인 『The reason why she plays the piano』 『Flowing Spring』 『I try to See Good-Bye on Your Back』, 안데르센의 『장미의 요정』 『바람이 들려주는 이야기』, 오스카 와일드의 『진지함의 중요성』

바라보는 대상이 된다는 것은
To be the object of gaze is to be

박효석 33번째 시집

오송숲

차례

◊ 시인의 말

1부

철 이른 봄 12
묵시록 14
봄의 배내옷 16
수다 떠는 봄 18
콩나물시루의 콩나물들 20
몸을 씻는 바다 22
간절함과 절절함 24
선인장 26
나무들의 겨울 외피 28
어머니의 홍시 같은 사랑 30
유리창 같은 경계 32
동안거(冬安居) 34

2부

물의 사막 38
외로움 40
문득, 42
사랑의 백치 44
실직자의 발걸음 46
둥글게 둥글게 48
지구의 날 50
과일 같은 황혼의 사랑 52
새들이 비상할 때마다 54
사랑꽃 56
그대를 위한 헌가(軒歌) 58
바라보는 대상이 된다는 것은 60
카리브해 2 62
아이스크림처럼 64

3부

아기의 눈물　68
사막 같은 세상일 때　70
언덕길을 오를 때면　72
배롱꽃을 보며　74
사랑의 부표　76
맥문동 꽃길 속을 거닐며　78
내 마음의 시계　80
가을무　82
연시처럼　84
만년설　86
끝물 사과　88
사랑한다는 것은　90
떠난다는 것은　92

4부

세월의 길 96
아직 병마개를 따지 않은 98
흙의 날 100
대파를 썰 때면 102
빈 의자 104
바닥1 106
바닥2 108
눈물 나는 나이 110
무명초의 세월 112
노후의 사랑 114
이름 없는 풀꽃에게 116
밝음과 어둠 118
너도 그렇다 120
가벼워진다는 것은 122
묵정밭 같은 마음에 124

시인의 말

  2024년 새봄을 맞아 33 시집을 출간하게 되어 여간 마음이 기쁜 게 아닙니다. 특히 이번 시집 출간을 앞두고 마음이 설레는 것은 나의 시를 영역으로 새롭게 탄생시켜 준 안인숙 여류시인과 함께 시집을 출간하게 되었기 때문일 것입니다.
  오랜 기간 나의 시를 영역하느라 심혈을 기울였을 안인숙 시인에게 무한한 감사를 드립니다.
  아무쪼록 이번 33 시집이 새로움으로 소망과 사랑을 함께 하는 시집이 되길 기원해 봅니다.

2024년 새봄을 맞아

박효석

Poet's Note

I am thrilled to announce the publication of my 33rd poetry collection in the spring of 2024. What brings me immense happiness, especially as we near the release of this collection, is teaming up with poet In Suk Ahn. She has provided a new viewpoint to my poetry through her English translations, offering fresh perspectives. I'm incredibly grateful to In Suk Ahn, who must have devoted considerable effort over a long period to translate my poetry into English.

I sincerely hope that this 33rd poetry collection will serve as a source of hope and love, offering novelty and freshness.

Hyo Seok Park

Spring of 2024

1부

철 이른 봄

봄이 오고 있는지
여인의 얼굴에 새순이 돋고 있다

겨우내 봄을 잉태하고 있었나보다

조산의 산기가 있었는지
철 이른 봄에 여인이 여리디여린
이른둥이를 낳고 있다

아직은 추운 겨울기가 가시지 않아
봄의 인큐베이터에서
철 이른 봄을 키우고 있는 여인

창밖에서
여인을 바라보려고 목을 삐끔 내밀던 산수유가
봄을 시샘하는 찬바람에
얼굴을 파묻고 있다

Early Spring

As spring approaches,
New shoots sprout on a woman's face

It seems as if she is conceiving spring during winter

There was a sign of premature birth
In the early spring, the woman is giving birth
To a tender and early child

While the lingering cold winter
Still refuses to leave,
The woman nurtures early spring
In the incubator of Spring

Outside the window,
A cornelian cherry blossom,
Extending its neck to catch a glimpse of the woman,
Is burying its face in the cold breeze
That's jealous of spring

묵시록

꽃들이
벌 나비들에게
얼마든지 꽃향기를 취해가도 좋다고
향기의 심장을 열어주듯이

그대는
나에게
얼마든지 사랑의 향기를 취해가도 좋다고
사랑의 심장을 열어주고 있네

The Silent Implication

As flowers
open the heart of fragrance
to the visiting butterflies and bees,
freely offering their fragrance,

You, my love,
open your heart to me,
allowing me to imbibe
the scent of your love.

봄의 배내옷

겨우내 떴던 스웨터의 실이
풀려나가듯이
아지랑이가 피어오르면

흙들이 굳었던 몸을 부드럽게 풀며
심호흡을 할 때마다
실개천에선 햇살이 명주실을 풀어가며
비단을 짜고 있는데

연초록 물레를 돌리며
봄의 배내옷을 열심히 만들고 있는
들과 산

Spring's Swaddling Clothes

Like the threads of a sweater
That knitted last winter unravels,
When spring haze rises,

The dirt softens its hardened body,
And every time it takes a deep breath
In the streamlet, the sun is unraveling the silk threads
And weaving silk.

Fields and mountains are
Spinning the spinning wheel in bright green
And are working hard to make
Spring's swaddling clothes.

수다 떠는 봄

겨우내 묵비권을 행사하던 나무와 꽃들이
봄이 오자
수다를 떨기 시작한다

땅 밑이나 돌덩어리 밑에서도
쥐 죽은 듯 움츠리고 있던 온갖 풀꽃들도
봄기운이 돌기 무섭게
기지개를 활짝 켜며 수다를 떨기 시작하는데

수다를 떨 때마다
따스한 입김이 서려 나와
땅이나 돌 틈이나 나무나 꽃잎에서
아지랑이가 피어오르는 봄

실개천도
겨우내 굳게 닫혀있던 마음을 활짝 열고
은빛 나게 수다를 떨며 흐른다

Chatting Spring

The trees and flowers,
Which had exercised their right of silence,
As spring arrives,
They begin to chat.

Even the various grasses and flowers
That were huddled underground or beneath the rocks
Seem to stretch and open up fiercely
And they start to chat,

Whenever they chat,
A warm breath comes up,
And in the gaps of the earth and rocks
Or on trees, and flower petals,
Spring haze emerges.

So the brooklet,
Opening up its tightly closed heart,
Flows while chatting with silver color.

콩나물시루의 콩나물들

콩나물시루에서
음표들이 쑥쑥 자라오른다

아침, 저녁으로
물을 주시는 어머니의 손길 따라
쑥쑥 자라오른 음표들이
화음을 다 맞춰보았는지
합창을 하기 시작하면

어머니는 이른 아침부터
아스파라긴산과 레시틴이 잘 우러나오는
음(音)이 될 수 있도록
음(音)을 교정하거나 편곡을 해가며
지휘를 하신다

가족들의 불편한 속이나
어지러운 머릿속을 맑게 해줄
합창을 들려주기 위하여
어머니는 이른 아침부터
지극정성 사랑으로
지휘를 하신다

Bean Sprout in the Jar

In the jar for growing bean sprouts,
Musical notes grow vigorously.

Guided by the gentle touch of my mother
Watering morning and evening,
The notes grow tall.
When they begin to sing in chorus
While harmonizing themselves,

From early morning,
My mother conducts with dedication,
Adjusting and arranging the notes
To become a melody filled with
Asparaginic acid and lecithin.

To clear the uncomfortable stomachs
And the dizzy minds of the family,
In the early morning,
With utmost love and sincerity,
My mother conducts the chorus.

몸을 씻는 바다

바다는 얼마나 큰 비누로
몸을 씻길래
쉴 새 없이 흰 거품이 밀려오는 것인지

흰 거품이 쉴 새 없이 밀려오고 있는
바다를 바라보고 있노라면
몸을 쉼 없이 깨끗이 닦아서인지
바다는 투명하기 이를 데 없는 에메랄드빛인데

자유자재 몸을 솟구치며 유영하고 있는 물고기들의 몸이
왜 그리도 싱싱하며
왜 그리도 갈매기들이 끊임없이 바다의 살갗을 스치며
날고 있는지를
바다를 바라보면 그 이유를 알 수 있을 것 같아

걸친 세상 옷을 훌훌 벗어 던지고
알몸이 되어
'첨벙' 바다에 뛰어든다

The Sea that Washes Its Body

How vast a soap does the sea use to cleanse itself,
Causing ceaselessly frothy waves to keep rushing in?

As I gaze upon the sea
Where the white foam incessantly rolls in,
Is it because the body is tirelessly scrubbed clean
That the sea appears transparent, an unparalleled emerald hue?

The bodies of fish, freely soaring and swimming,
Why are they so vibrant and alive,
And why do seagulls tirelessly skim the skin of the sea,
Flapping their wings without end?
Looking at the sea, I feel like finding the answer,

Shedding all the clothes of the world,
And becoming naked,
I plunge into the sea, *Splash!*

간절함과 절절함

아름다운 꽃들을 바라보고 있노라면
향기로운 사랑의 향내가
온몸을 감싸오듯이
꽃이 아름답게 꽃폈다는 것은
절절함이 만발하였다는 것 같아
그대의 간절한 목숨 같은 사랑 또한
절절함의 향내가 내 몸을 감싸오듯
그윽하여라

생애 한 번 최고의
사랑의 향기로
간절히 꽃피고 싶은 절절함이여

Earnest Desire and the Eagerness

When gazing at beautiful flowers,
As the fragrant scent of love
Envelopes my entire being,
The blossoming of flowers in all their beauty
Seems to embody profound intensity.
Also, your earnest and ardent love,
Of which a poignant fragrance embraces me,
Is deep and gentle.

In their one lifetime,
They have a yearning to bloom
With the utmost fragrance of the greatest love,
Oh, the fervor and the eagerness.

선인장

선인장은 아름다운 꽃을 피우기 위해
온몸에 가시가 돋는 아픔을
참아내고 있는가 보다

물 한 모금 고이지 않는
길도 보이지 않는 막막한 사막에서
시도 때도 없이 휘몰아치는 모래 폭풍이나
용광로같이 활활 불타는 화염을
온몸으로 견뎌내며
끝끝내 아름다운 꽃을 피워내고 있는 걸 보면

선인장은 아마도 첫사랑의 황홀한 꿈을
목숨으로 꾸고 있는
사막의 사랑 화신인가 보다

Cactus

The cactus might endure the pain of sharp thorns
All over its body to bloom beautiful flowers.

In the desolate desert
Where not even a sip of water doesn't stagnate
And a path is nowhere in sight,
It withstands the relentless onslaught of sandstorms,
Much like a volcanic blaze,
Enduring the flames with its entire being.

Witnessing it bloomed beautiful flowers in the end,
The cactus is perhaps akin to a desert deity of love,
Earnestly dreaming the enchanting dream of first love
With its very life.

나무들의 겨울 외피

겨울이면 나무들의 외피가
노동으로 굳은살이 박인
노동자들의 손바닥같이 되는 것은

갖은 난관에도
가족들을 먹여 살리기 위하여
꿋꿋이 이겨내고 있는
노동자들의 의지처럼
어떠한 한파가 몰아쳐 온다 해도
돌아오는 새봄의 새 생명의 순을 틔워주기 위해서라면
온몸으로 견뎌 내겠다는
굳은 의지의 결집이 아닐는지

한파가 몰아칠수록
더욱 찬바람이 집안 내부 속으로 들어올 수 없도록
노동자들의 굳은살로 결집하고 있는
나무들의 겨울 외피

The Winter Bark of Trees

In winter, the outer layer of trees,
much like the calloused palms of laborers
hardened through toil, endures.

Just like laborers' strong will,
facing numerous hardships,
persistently overcome challenges
to provide for their families,
no matter how a harsh cold sweeps in,
to give rise to buds of new life in the coming spring,
it seems these trees are determined
to withstand and endure, akin to
the unwavering will of laborers.

As the cold intensifies,
to prevent the chilling winds,
the trees bind together with their toughened bark,
a resolute cohesion akin to laborers' callus.

어머니의 홍시 같은 사랑

고향에 홀로 남아 계신
어머니를 생각하면
바람이 불 때마다 떨어질라
온 힘으로 매달려 있으면서
배고픈 까치의 밥이 되길
기다리고 있는 홍시처럼
자나 깨나 자식들에게 마지막 남은 생명까지도
다 주고 이 세상을 떠날 수 있길
애타게 소원하고 계신 어머니의 모습이 떠올라

홍시를 먹을 때면
빛깔 곱게 잘 익은 어머니의 사랑을 먹는 것만 같아
홍시가 달랑 한 개 달려있는 고향집으로
까치가 되어 날아가고 싶은데

자꾸만 홍시가 떨어지고 있는 듯한 소리가
들려오고 있는 고향집

Love like Mother's Soft Ripe Persimmons

When I think of my mother,
Staying alone in my hometown,
Like a ripe persimmon,
Hoping to become a hungry magpie's food,
Since every time the wind blows,
It feels like it might fall,
Hanging on with all its strength,
Wishing fervently that even the last remaining life
Could be given to her children,
And leaving this world,
Which is the image of my mother,
Longing desperately for such a wish.

Because whenever I eat soft persimmons,
I feel like I'm eating mother's love, ripe with color,
I wish to become a magpie and fly to
My hometown house
Where just one persimmon is hanging.

I hear the sound of persimmons falling one by one,
Resonating through my hometown house.

유리창 같은 경계

유리창은 안과 밖을 다 볼 수 있지만
안과 밖을 나누고 있는 경계인 것처럼
하나도 숨김없이 들여다볼 수 있다는 것이
경계가 될 줄은
당신이나 나나 그때는
꿈에도 정말 몰랐었던 것 같습니다.

나는 당신이고
당신은 곧 나라고 믿어질 만큼
우린 하나라고 생각했었기에
그때는 상대에 대한 궁금한 호기심이 계속 있어야
관심이 이어진다는 사실을
우린 정말 생각조차 못 했었던 것 같습니다

만일 당신과 나 사이에
그때도 유리창 같은 경계가 있었더라면
지금, 이 순간에도 안에 있는 사람은
계속 밖을 내다보려고 할 것이고
밖에 있는 사람은
끊임없이 안을 들여다보려고 하지 않을까요

The Glass-like Boundary

A glass window allows one to see
Both inside and outside,
Yet, like the boundary
Separating the interior and exterior,
It seems we never knew back then
The thing we can see everything each other through
Could be a boundary.

I am you,
And as much as I believe you are very me.
Once believed we were one,
Little did we realize that
We need to be curious about each other
To keep the interest going.

Between you and me,
If there had been the glass-like boundary,
At this very moment,
The one inside would continue to gaze outward,
And the one outside would continuously peer within,
Don't you think?

동안거(冬安居)

겨울에 접어들면서
나무들이 그동안 가을 정취에 물들어 있던
나뭇잎들을 다 떨궈내며
알몸이 되고 있는 것을 바라보니
마치 동안거에 들어가는 스님들 같아
아무쪼록 겨울을 잘 수행하고 나와
새봄에 새잎을 틔우는 나무들이 되길
기원해 본다

혹독한 겨울을 고행하고 나면
나이테가 하나 더 생긴 굵어진 몸통으로
세상을 더 높이 더 멀리 가지들을 뻗게 하여
연초록 새잎을 눈이 부시게 틔워줄 것이라고 생각하니
나도 겨울 동안 동안거에 들어가
고행을 감당해야겠다는 생각을 해본다

욕망과 세속을 벗어 던진 알몸으로
냉철히 내면을 들여다보면서
내 본연의 모습을 찾을 때까지
수행해야겠다는 생각을 해본다

The Winter Zen Retreat (冬安居)

As winter approaches,
Trees shed leaves
That had been colored by the autumn atmosphere,
Leaving themselves bare.
Observing this,
It feels like monks entering the winter Zen retreat,
Wishing to endure the winter successfully
And become trees that bloom
With new leaves in the coming spring.

After enduring a harsh winter,
With tree rings and a thick trunk,
They will extend their branches higher and farther,
Gracefully adorning the early spring
With dazzling new leaves,
I contemplate entering the winter Zen retreat,
Enduring the hardships.

Stripping away desires and worldly attachments,
Examining the inner self with a naked honesty,
I think I will do practice until I rediscover my true self.

2부

물의 사막

바다를 바라보면
내 마음이 수평선에 가 머문다

그 임을 그리워하는 그리움도
수평선에 가 머문다

수평선을 바라보고 있노라면
망망한 바다의 종착지가 꼭 그곳일 것만 같아
언제 그 종착지에 도달할 수 있을는지
바라보면 바라볼수록
수평선은 망망한 물의 사막
그리움의 오아시스 같은데

그 임에 대한 그리움이 절절하면 절절할수록
내 마음도 해돋이와 해넘이로 그곳에 가 머물면서
수평선의 오아시스가 되고 있는
물의 사막

The Desert of Water

When I gaze upon the sea,
My heart lingers on the horizon.

The yearning for you
Too lingers at the horizon.

While gazing at the horizon,
The destination of the vast sea seems so near,
I wonder when it can be reached by mere observation.
As I gaze at it repeatedly,
The horizon resembles
A vast and endless desert of water,
An oasis of yearning.

As the longing for you becomes intense,
My heart also stays there
With the sunrise and the sunset,
Becoming an oasis of the water desert on the horizon.

외로움

외로움은 유배된 무인도 같아
망망한 바다를 하염없이 바라보듯
수신 불명이어라

Loneliness

Loneliness feels like
Being on a deserted island in exile.
Just like gazing endlessly at the vast, desolate sea,
Lost in the signal of connection.

문득,

살아가다 보면 갑자기
옛일이 생각날 때가 있다

아득하게 잊어버린 것만 같았던 옛일이
무심코 노상 가던 길이 아니라
얼떨결에 낯선 새로운 길에 들어섰을 때의
준비 안 된 호기심처럼
두리번거리다가는 어디선가 본 것만 같은
낯익은 옛집 같은 집을 발견하였을 때의
오래도록 잊고 살았던 옛일이
갑자기 생각을 지배하는 것은
그리움일까

살아가다 보면
늘 가던 길을 갑자기 되돌아오게 하거나
나도 모르는 새 샛길로 가게 하다가는
급작스럽게 발길을 멈추게 하는

문득,
머리를 스치는
옛집 같은 사랑

Suddenly,

As I live, there are moments
When memories of the past come flooding back.

Things that seemed to have been totally forgotten
Like the unprepared curiosity
When stepping onto a new path,
Not the familiar road I used to tread,
But an unfamiliar one in an unguarded moment,
When wandering, stumbling upon
A house that seems oddly familiar,
The old memories that I had long forgotten,
Suddenly dominating my thoughts,
Is it longing?

As I journey through life,
It may suddenly make me come back
From the usual path
Or lead me down to an unknown byway,
Which makes me halt abruptly.

Suddenly,
The old house-like love
Flashing through my mind.

사랑의 백치

백지는 때론 백치 같아서
백지를 펼쳐놓았을 때
눈앞이 캄캄할 때가 많다

무엇을 채워야 할지
도무지 감이 오지 않을 때
눈앞이 하얗다거나
눈앞이 깜깜하다는
표현을 쓰고 있는 걸 보면

하얀 것을 검은 것이라고 말해도 되고
검은 것을 하얀 것이라고 말해도 되는 것 같아서
백지 펼쳐 놓은 것을
흑지 펼쳐 놓았다고 말해도 상관없는
아득하기만 하여 감이 오지 않는
백지를 펼쳐놓고는

그대에게 어떤 말로 사랑의 고백을 시작해야 할지
한 자도 진척하지 못하고 낑낑거리고 있을 때면
눈앞이 캄캄해지거나
눈앞이 하얗게 되는
사랑의 백치

The Fool of Love

A blank sheet, at times, just like a fool,
When unfolded,
The moment I am often plunged into darkness.

When unsure of what to fill in,
And inspiration refuses to come,
Expressions like 'the sight turning white'
Or 'the sight turning pitch black'
May be used interchangeably.

It seems as though it doesn't matter
Whether the unfolded sheet is called blank or black,
Unfolding it,
I don't know just what to say.

When struggling to initiate a confession of love to you,
Unable to make any progress,
The moment may either darken or whiten
In front of my sight,
I am the fool of love.

실직자의 발걸음

일터가 있는 사람들의 발걸음은
길을 걸을 때
해돋이의 맑은 햇살이 세상을 두루 비추듯이
땅을 딛는 힘이 경쾌한 데 반해
일터가 없는 실직자들의 발걸음은
마치 서산마루로 뉘엿뉘엿 넘어가고 있는
해거름 같아

집에 귀가하지도 못하고
수평선 너머로
산봉우리 너머로
꼴깍~

어둠 속에 묻히고 마는
실직자의 발걸음

The Steps of the Unemployed

The footsteps of those with jobs,
as they walk the path,
are as lively as the clear sunlight of dawn,
illuminating the world all around,
and the strength in their steps feels invigorating.

In contrast, the footsteps of the unemployed
are like a sunset,
slowly sliding down the slope over the west ridge.

Unable to return home,
beyond the horizon,
over the peaks of mountains,
Falling~

Buried within the darkness,
the steps of the unemployed
fade away.

둥글게 둥글게

원 식탁에 앉아 식사할 때면
우리 식구들의 마음은 둥근 원이 된다

지구가 둥글다는 것으로부터 시작해서
둥근 얼굴은 웃는 얼굴이라는 등
둥글게 둥글게 살자며
음식을 맛있게 먹으며 행복한 웃음을 짓는다

식탁이 원 식탁이듯
행복한 웃음이 원을 이루면
식탁에 차려진 음식들을 건강한 숨으로
모난 시간이나 각진 시간들을
잘 삭이고 소화시켜 가면서
둥근 지구에선 둥글게 둥글게 살아가야 한다며
행복의 팡파르를 둥글도록 울린다

Round and Round

When sitting at a round dining table,
The hearts of our family become like a circle.

Starting from the fact that the Earth is round,
To the idea that a round face is a smiling face,
Let us live roundly, roundly,
Enjoying delicious meals and sharing joyful laughter.

Just as the table is round,
When the laughter forms a circle of happiness,
The foods on the table, like a healthy breath,
Properly digest and assimilate
Rough or angular times,
Resonating with the roundness of life
On this round Earth,
Playing the fanfare with joy.

지구의 날

지구의 생일날을 맞아
난 거리에 버려진 휴지와 담배꽁초를 줍는다

내가 휴지와 담배꽁초를 주우면
그 자리의 지구의 피부병이 깨끗이 날 것만 같아
지구의 생일을 축하하는 선물로
지구 나이만큼의 민들레꽃 홀씨를
그 자리로 날려 보낸다

민들레꽃들이
그 자리에서 앙증맞게 꽃피기를 간절히 기원하며
지구 나이만큼의 민들레꽃 홀씨를
날려 보낸다

On Earth Day

To celebrate the birthday of our planet,
I roam the streets
Picking up garbage and cigarette butts.

When I pick up garbage and cigarette butts,
I feel I am cleansing the Earth's skin right there,
As a gift to celebrate Earth's birthday,
I scatter dandelion seeds equal to the Earth's age
To send them off to that spot.

I wish the dandelion seeds
Blossom right there charmingly,
Scattering dandelion seeds equal to the Earth's age,
Sending them off into the air.

과일 같은 황혼의 사랑

풋풋하고 싱싱했던 과일들이
일기 불순의 시간들을 온몸으로 익혀가면서
잘 익은 빛깔 고운 과일로 변해가듯이
너와 나의 사랑 또한 그러하려니

파란만장했던 질곡의 세월들을
오로지 생명처럼 사랑을 익혀가면서
인생 말년에 빛깔 고운 노을로 물들이고 있는
황혼 같은 사랑을 지긋이 바라보며
미소 짓고 있는 너와 내가 될지어니

우리의 사랑아
이 세상에서 가장 향긋하고 빛깔 곱게 익어가는
과일 같은 황혼이 되거라

Twilight Love like Fruits

Once fruits were fresh and vibrant,
Which ripened through the uneven moments,
Transforming into beautifully ripe and radiant colors,
So shall our love, you and I.

Through the tumultuous years
Filled with varied experiences,
Nurturing our love like the essence of life,
In the twilight of our lives,
Painting it with the hues of a refined sunset,
Gazing affectionately
At the love resembling the twilight,
Smiling, you and I may become.

Oh, our love,
Become the most fragrant and gracefully ripening
Twilight love like fruits.

새들이 비상할 때마다

땅에 앉아있던 새들이
하늘을 향해 비상할 때마다
땅 위로 새들의 검은 그림자가
날아가고 있는 것을 보면

살아있는 동안
쉴 새 없이 하늘을 향해 비상하다가
수명이 다 되고 나면
결국은 땅에 묻힐 운명이라는 것을
예고하는 것만 같은데

땅에 앉아있던 새들이
하늘을 향해 비상할 때마다
하늘과 땅은 떼려야 뗄 수 없는
어찌할 수 없는 숙명의 관계라는 것을
몸으로 이야기라도 하는 듯이
땅을 훑듯이 날아가고 있는
검은 그림자의 새들

Whenever the Birds Take Flight

Whenever the birds that were resting on the ground
Take flight towards the sky,
As I witness the black shadows of the birds
Soaring upwards, leaving the ground behind,

It seems to foretell
They ascent towards the sky unceasingly,
And if their lifespan comes to an end,
They are destined to be buried
In the ground inevitably.

Whenever the birds, once perched upon the ground,
Take flight towards the sky,
They seem to tell us
As if the sky and the ground are inseparably bound,
The shadowed birds in flight,
Flying over close to the ground.

사랑꽃

삶이 아무리 고달프고 힘들지라도
사랑꽃이 피면
더없이 행복하여라

가진 것이라곤 마음과 몸뿐일 때도
사랑꽃이 피면
아낌없이 마음과 몸을 다 내어줄 수 있어
한없이 행복하여라

사랑꽃이 피면
한 치 앞도 내다볼 수 없는 냉골 같은 아득함도
사랑의 기쁨의 눈물이 뜨거운 온천처럼 솟구치며
사랑에 살고 사랑에 죽어도 좋다는 마음이
따뜻하게 품어주고 있어
한없이 행복하여라

며칠 남지 않은 시한부 목숨일 때도
사랑꽃이 피면
부활의 생명수를 마시듯 사랑꽃 향기를 마시며
육신은 죽어도 영(靈)은 사랑으로 부활할 수 있다는
기쁨이 차고 넘쳐흘러
더없이 행복하여라

Love Flower

No matter how arduous and challenging life may be,
When the love flower blooms, be infinitely happy.

Even when all you have is your heart and body,
When the love flower blooms,
You can generously give your heart and body
Without hesitation, be endlessly happy.

When the love flower blooms,
Even the distant and cold uncertainty of the future
Is embraced warmly
By the tears of joy like a hot spring
And the feeling that it's okay to live and die for love,
Be endlessly happy.

Even when facing the end of a limited life,
When the love flower blooms,
Drinking in the fragrance of the love flower
Like the water of resurrection,
Overflowing with happiness which feeling the joy
That the spirit can resurrect with love,
Be endlessly happy.

그대를 위한 헌가(軒歌)

사람이 꽃처럼 아름답다고 말하지 말고
꽃이 사람처럼 아름답다고 말하라

그대가 주어(主語)라면
꽃은 나에게
그대를 위한 수식어에 불과하나니

그대를 꽃처럼 향기롭다고 말하지 말고
꽃이 그대처럼 향기롭다고 말하라

Ode for You

Rather than saying a person is beautiful like a flower,
Say that a flower is beautiful like a person.

If you are the subject,
Then the flower, to me,
Is nothing but an adjective for you.

Instead of claiming you are fragrant like a flower,
Say that the flower is fragrant like you.

바라보는 대상이 된다는 것은

바라보는 대상이 된다는 것은
그대가 아름답기 때문이다

바라보는 대상이 된다는 것은
그대가 향긋하기 때문이다

바라보는 대상이 된다는 것은
그대로 하여금 꿈을 꿀 수 있기 때문이다

바라보는 대상이 된다는 것은
멀리 바라보이는 수평선으로
꿈결 같은 물결들이 다가가듯이
사랑하고픈 마음으로
그대에게 다가가고 싶기 때문이다

To be the object of gaze is to be

To be the object of gaze
Is because of your beauty

To be the object of gaze
Is because of your fragrance

To be the object of gaze
Is because you allow dreams to unfold

To be the object of gaze is to be
Because I want to approach you
With a heart full of love,
Just as dreamlike waves
Approach the distant horizon

카리브해 2

카리브해에는
해가 뜨고 해가 지는
해의 길을 따라
에메랄드빛 바다 밑이 투명하게 드러나는
금사(金絲)길이 열리고 있다

그 길을 따라가면
해가 뜨고 해가 지듯
사후(死後), 나도 그럴 수 있을까

해안에 서서 빠질 듯이 금사(金絲)길을 바라보며
피안으로 가고 있는 카리브해

The Caribbean Sea 2

In the Caribbean,
Where the sun rises and sets,
Along the path of the sun,
Beneath the emerald sea,
A golden silk road is unveiled,
Transparently revealing the sea world below.

Following that path,
As if the sun rises and sets,
In the afterlife,
Could I also experience such moments?

Standing on the coast,
Gazing as if sinking into the golden silk road,
Entering an enlightened state
By the Caribbean Sea.

아이스크림처럼

당신의 사랑은
아이스크림처럼 달콤하고 부드러워서
언제나 내 마음에 스르르 녹아들지요

아무리 찜통 같은 무더위로
내 마음을 쫙쫙 갈라지게 가뭄 들게 하여도
당신의 사랑은 달콤하고 부드러운 아이스크림 같아서
언제나 내 마음에 눈 녹듯이 스르르 녹아들지요

당신의 사랑이 언제나 내 마음에
달콤하고 부드럽게 스르르 녹아들 수 있는 것은
남극이나 북극의 빙하처럼
당신의 사랑을 꽁꽁 얼어버리게 하는데도 불구하고
당신은 나를 위하여
늘 아낌없이 녹아들 준비를 하고 있기에
언제나 당신의 사랑은
달콤하고 부드러운 아이스크림처럼
눈 녹듯이 스르르 내 마음에 녹아들지요

Like Ice Cream

Your love,
Like sweet and tender ice cream,
Melts into my heart as always.

Even when the scorching heat
Causes my heart to crack and split,
Your love, like sweet and tender ice cream,
Always melts into my heart like snow.

The reason your love can always
Sweetly and gently melt into my heart
Is because,
Even though I freeze your love completely,
Like the glaciers of the North or South Pole,
You, for me,
Are always ready to thaw without hesitation.
So, always, your love,
Like sweet and tender ice cream,
Melts into my heart like melting snow.

3부

아기의 눈물은

아기의 눈물은
연초록 풀잎을 흐르고 있는
이슬방울 같아

아기가 울면
풀벌레들이 운다

Baby's tears

Baby's tears
Resemble dewdrops
Flowing on light green leaves

When a baby cries
Grass bugs weep

사막 같은 세상일 때

세상을 살아가다 사막 같은 세상일 때
아득하리만치 길도 보이지 않는 사막에서
온몸에 가시 박힌 채로 뿌리를 내리고 살고 있는
선인장을 생각하라

허구한 날 살인적인 폭염과
온몸을 휩쓸고 가는 모래 폭풍 속에서도
아주 드물게 비라도 올라치면
온몸으로 물 한 방울 생명수처럼 지켜가며
허허벌판 사막에서
목숨을 다해가며 아름다운 꽃을 피우고 있는
선인장을 생각하라

마치 가시 면류관을 쓴 예수와 같이
사방천지 길도 보이지 않는
물 한 방울 고여 있지 않은 사막에서
온몸이 가시투성이가 되도록
최상의 아름다운 사막의 꽃을 피우고 있는
선인장을 생각하라

In a World like a Desert

When feeling living in the world like a desert,
In a vast expanse where the path
Is nowhere to be seen,
Think of the cactus living with roots down
Pierced all over the body with thorns.

Under the murderous scorching heat,
Even in the sandstorm that sweeps the body,
If rain happens to fall very rarely,
It protects its own life
Preserving a drop of water in its way
With the whole body in the vast desert.
So, think of the cactus blooming beautiful flowers
With all its might.

Like Jesus wearing a crown made of thorns,
In every direction, where no roads are visible,
In a desert where not a drop of water is stored,
Even with the body covered in thorns,
Think of the cactus flowering
The finest and most beautiful desert flowers.

언덕길을 오를 때면

언덕길을 오를 때면
언덕길에 피어있는 들풀꽃들을 바라보며
힘을 내며 오른다

평지와 다름없이 언덕길에서도 주어진 운명을
최선을 다해 피고 있는 들풀꽃들을
바라보고 있노라면
땡볕과 비바람 속에서도
하루도 빠짐없이 길가에 좌판을 깔아놓고는
생계를 이어가느라
삶의 언덕길을 목숨을 걸듯이 오르고 있는
노점상들의 억척스런 삶의 체취가
풍겨오는 것만 같아

언덕길을 오를 때면
들풀꽃들을 바라보며
한 걸음 한 걸음 있는 힘을 다해가며 오른다

When Climbing Up the Hill

When climbing up the hill,
Gazing at the wildflowers blooming along the hillside,
I ascend with strength.

If I gaze at the wildflowers striving to give their best
Despite their destined fate, striving to bloom
I feel like the tenacious scent of life
From the street vendors
Wafts through the air,
Displaying their wares every day
Under the scorching sun
And in the gusty winds,
Continuously sustaining their livelihoods,
Climbing the hill of life with their lives at stake.

When climbing up the hill,
Gazing at the wildflowers,
I ascend, step by step, with all the strength I have.

배롱꽃을 보며

열사병 같은 화염을
안으로 삭이고 삭여
아름다운 불꽃 같은 꽃으로 꽃 피우고 있는
배롱꽃을 보고 있노라면

세상의 화병(火病) 같은 열병을
평생 속으로 삭여가며
아름다운 사랑의 꽃으로 꽃 피우셨던
어머님의 얼굴이 떠올라

배롱꽃 향기에 코를 묻는다

Gazing at the Crape Myrtle Flowers

When I watch the crape myrtle flowers
Calming the heatstroke-like flame down,
Blooming as splendidly as flames,

It reminds me of my mother's face,
Who bloomed wide with the exquisite flower of love,
While extinguishing her inner fever
Akin to hypochondria in her lifetime.

I bury my nose
In the fragrance of the crape myrtle flowers.

사랑의 부표

사막에서 망망한 대해(大海)의 부표 같은
오아시스를 찾아 헤매듯이
세상에서 나의 사랑을 찾아 헤매다가
당신을 만나 평생을 살아보니
살아가면 살아갈수록
당신이 그렇게도 내가 죽을 듯이 찾아 헤매던
사랑의 부표 같은 오아시스였다는 걸
행복이 젖어 들듯이 알게 되었지요

당신을 만나기 전에는
모래바람으로 가득 찼던 내 마음이
당신과 함께 살면서
꽃밭의 꽃들이 짓고 있는 아름다운 행복의 미소처럼
당신의 사랑으로 정수되어
사랑의 부표 같은 오아시스의 맑은 샘물이 되고 있다는 걸
알게 되었지요

Love's Buoy

Like a buoy on the vast sea in the desert,
As if searching for an oasis,
I wandered in search of my love in this world.
Upon meeting and sharing a lifetime with you,
As my life goes on,
I realized, permeated with happiness,
That you are the oasis, like a buoy of love,
Where I had been desperately searching for.

Before meeting you,
My heart was filled with sandstorms,
But now I know,
As I've been living with you,
Like the beautiful smiles of flowers in the garden,
Refined by your love,
Becoming a clear spring of the oasis,
Like a buoy of love.

맥문동 꽃길 속을 거닐며

불사초인 맥문동이 보라 꽃을 피울 때면
이 세상을 몽땅 비우시고
저세상으로 떠나시느라 안간힘을 쓰시던
어머니의 영(靈)이
꽃으로 피어나고 있는 것 같아

보라 꽃길 속을 거닐면 거닐수록
이 세상에서의 마지막 작별 같은 엷은 미소를
입가에 드리우시곤
모진 이 세상을 다 비우신 걸 보여 주시느라
항문을 활짝 열어 보여주시던 어머니처럼
어쩌면 맥문동 보라 꽃도
추운 겨울의 항문을 활짝 열어
꽃으로 피운 것이 아닌가 하는 생각이 들어

맥문동 보라 꽃길 속을 거닐며
추운 이 세상을 비워가고 있는
나의 항문

Stroll through the path of Lilyturf Flowers

When the immortal grass, Lilyturf, blossoms,
I feel like my mother's spirit,
Who was trying so hard to leave this world,
Emptying this whole world
And blossoming into a flower.

The more I walk through the purple flowers,
The more I think that my mother,
With a thin smile like the last farewell in this world.
To show me that she has emptied herself
Of this harsh world,
Like my mother, who opened her anus wide to show,
Maybe the violet Lilyturf flower opened her anus wide
In the cold winter and bloomed into flowers.

Strolling through the violet Lilyturf trail,
My anus is emptying this cold world.

내 마음의 시계

보고픈 사람과 약속이 있는 날이면
내 마음은 시계가 된다

'째깍' '째깍'
내 마음속에서 쉴 새 없이 돌아가고 있는 시곗바늘을
약속 시간 가까이 돌려놓았다가는
다시 제시간으로 되돌려 놓기를 반복하며
시간이 흐르는 사이사이
보고픈 사람과의 지난날의 아름다웠던 시간들을 떠올리면
입가에 핀 미소의 꽃에서
보고픈 사람으로부터의 향긋한 향내가 풍겨온다

보고픔이 간절해지면 간절해질수록
속도위반하는 것쯤은
눈 하나 깜짝 안 하는가 보다

속도위반을 밥 먹듯 하면서
약속 시간에 가닿기를 반복하고 있는 걸 보면
내 마음의 시계는 온전히
보고픔의 숨 쉼에 따라
초침이 돌아가고 있는가 보다

My Heart's Clock

On day when I have a promise to meet someone
I miss, my heart becomes a clock.

Tock Tick inside my heart,
The clock hands are constantly turning,
Adjusting them close to the promised time,
Repeating the process of setting them back
To the right time,
In the intervals as time passes,
Recalling the beautiful moments
With the person I miss,
From the flower of a smile blooming on my lips,
A fragrant scent of the person I miss wafts.

As the yearning intensifies,
And as it becomes more fervent,
I don't even bat my eyes about speeding.

Recklessly exceeding the speed limit,
Repeating the act of reaching the agreed-upon time,
It seems my heart's clock is entirely
Turning its second hand
In sync with my breath of yearning.

가을무

가을무의 살결이 하얗고 매끈한 것을 보면
땅속에 묻혀서 자라는 동안
하늘에서 내려주는 비를
샘물 같은 물로 정수하여
마음결이 보드랍고 시원하도록 마시며
자랐기 때문인가 보다

김장을 담가 겨우내 먹는 사람들에게
아무리 세상이 꽁꽁 언다 할지라도
겨우내 샘물 같은 시원한 물로 마음을 정수하면서
흰 눈 같은 하얀 마음으로
겨울을 보낼 수 있게 하기 위하였기 때문인가 보다

Autumn Radish

Looking at the smooth and white skin
Of the Autumn radish,
Perhaps it's because it grew buried in the ground,
Drawing nourishment
From the rain sent down from the sky,
Filtering it like spring water
To make its mind pure and refreshing.

For those who make it Kimchi for winter consumption,
It is because
No matter how harshly the world may freeze,
Purifying with the cool water like spring water,
Allowing them to spend winter with a mind
As pure and white as snow.

연시처럼

연시를 먹을 때면
근근이 버티고 살아온 근간이 날아갈 것 같은 태풍과
힘겹게 쌓아온 세월의 둑이 터져버릴 것 같은 장마와
쉴 새 없이 우레 치는 시련 속에서도
땡감 같은 세월을 사랑으로 품어 안아
연시처럼 빛깔 곱게 잘 익은 생애를
하나도 남김없이 자식들에게 다 먹여주시고는
이 세상을 떠나실 때도
서녘 하늘을 연시 같은 고운 빛으로 물들이며 떠나시던
어머니가 떠올라

연시를 먹을 때면
잘 익은 연시처럼
나의 마음을 곱게 물들이고 있는
어머니의 사랑

Just Like Ripe Persimmons

Whenever eating ripe persimmons,
In a storm that could blow away the foundations
she had resiliently clung to,
And in the pouring rain, the levee of the years
She had painstakingly built might burst,
And even in the relentless trials
Where thunder roars without a break,
Embracing the years
Akin to the unripe persimmon with love,
And gave all to her children,
Which reminds me of my mother who,
When leaving this world,
Colored the western sky
With a delicate light like a ripe persimmon.

When I eat ripe persimmons,
Like a well-ripened persimmon,
My heart is gracefully dyed
With the love of my mother.

만년설

나의 세월을 입관할 때가 다가올수록
머리의 만년설이
백설로 휘날린다

세월을 하산하기 시작하여
하산 도착점 근방에 이르면 이를수록
머리의 만년설은
반대로 정점에 다가가듯이
백설로 휘날리고 있는 것을 보면

나의 세월을 화장(火葬)할 때
하얀 연기가 되어
하늘로 올라가려고 준비하고 있는 것이 아닌가 하는
생각이 들어
머리의 만년설이 가뿐하게 하늘로 올라갈 수 있도록
히말라야의 산 정상에서 푸른 하늘을 바라보듯이
세속을 날려버린다

Permanent Snow

As the time approaches to lay my years in a coffin,
The permanent snow on my head
Flutters like white snow.

Descending through the years,
Approaching the vicinity of the descent's destination,
The permanent snow on my head seems to flutter
As if reaching the pinnacle in reverse.

When I cremate my years,
The thought occurs that
The white smoke is ready to ascend to the sky,
So that the permanent snow on my head
Effortlessly could ascend to the sky,
As if gazing at the blue sky
From the summit of the Himalayas,
I cast the earthly away.

끝물 사과

끝물 사과를 따고 난 과수원이
해넘이가 넘어간 수평선처럼 고요하다

끝물 사과의 맛을 상큼하고 향긋하게
해넘이한 사과들이
수평선 너머에서 해돋이를 꿈꾸고 있듯
고요하기 그지없는 과수원의 사과나무들처럼

끝물 사과를 먹을 때면
빛깔 고운 싱싱한 해돋이를
온몸에 주렁주렁 달기 위한 꿈을 꾸고 있듯이
끝물 사과의 상큼하고 향긋한 맛이
온몸으로 번지고 있는
나의 해넘이

Last Apples of the Season

The orchard where the last apples are picked is
As serene as the horizon where the sun has set.

Like the apples from the last branches
- crisp and fragrant,
The apples from the horizon, beyond the line of sight,
Seem to dream of the sunrise,
As tranquil as the apple trees within the orchard.

When eating the last apples,
As if dreaming of draping the bright and fine sunrise
All over the body,
The crisp and fragrant flavor of the last-fruit apples
Spreads all over my body where my sun has set.

사랑한다는 것은

사랑한다는 것은
가슴에 꽃을 피우는 일이다

그대를 사랑하는 마음이
이 세상에서 가장 향기로운 사랑의 향기가 될 때까지
사랑한다는 것은
심장 안에 사랑의 꽃을 피우는 일이다

이 세상에 단 한 송이밖에 없는
천국 같은 꽃을
목숨으로 꽃피우는 일이다

To Love

To love is
To bloom a flower in my heart.

When the feeling of loving you
Becomes the most fragrant aroma of love
In this world,
To love is
To bloom a flower of love in my heart.

There is only one flower
Like a paradise in this world,
The act of making the flower bloom
With all my heart.

떠난다는 것은

떠난다는 것은
일상을 그리워하기 위함이다

무미건조하다고 느꼈던 일상들을
새록새록 그리워하기 위함이다

당연히 그 자리에 있겠거니 하고
생각했던 일상들이
하나둘씩 그 자리에서 보이지 않게 되면
그 빈자리의 일상들이
불현듯이 사무치게 그리워지듯이

떠난다는 것은
당연하다고 생각했었던 일상의 사랑들이
무인도를 외롭지 않도록
밤낮없이 어루만져주고 있는
바다의 물낯 같은
세상의 사랑이었음을 돌아보게 하기 위함이다

Leaving Is

Leaving is
In order to long for the everyday.

It is to newly yearn for the mundane moments
That once felt dry and flavorless.

The everyday occurrences, presumed to be there,
Slowly disappear one by one,
And as the everyday vacancies start to show,
They become unexpectedly and intensely missed,

Leaving is
You to reflect that everyday love, deemed natural
And taken for granted,
Is the world's great love for you,
Just like the persistent embrace of the sea,
Day or night,
So that an uninhabited island doesn't feel lonely.

4부

세월의 길

노부부가 손을 잡고 길을 걸을 때면
살아온 세월들이 꽃으로 피어나고 있는지
얼굴에 살포시 드리운 미소가
향기롭다

걷는 길이 점점 버거워져만 가는
얼마 남지 않은 세월의 길을
지금까지 희로애락을 한마음으로 동행한 그 마음으로
함께 손을 잡고 걷고 있는
노부부를 바라보고 있노라면

활짝 핀 사랑의 꽃향기가
은은하게 미소 짓고 있는
세월의 길

Path of the Years

When an elderly couple holds hands and walks,
It seems as if the years
They've lived blossom into flowers,
The gently spread smile on their faces is fragrant.

As the path they walk becomes increasingly not easy,
On the road of the twilight years,
Looking at the elderly couple walking hand in hand,
Who have shared joys and sorrows
With one heart until now,

The wide-open fragrance of love's flower
Is delicately smiling,
Along the path of the years.

아직 병마개를 따지 않은

빈 술병이 아니라
아직 병마개를 따지 않은,

슬픔이 가득 찼거나 기쁨이 넘쳐나는 술병이
친구나 연인처럼 다가와
병마개를 딸 수 있도록 함께 하여 준다면
존재감이 몸속을 타고 흘러
슬플 때나 기쁠 때나
생동감이 살아 숨 쉬는
술병이 될 수 있을 텐데

존재감의 효소가 알맞은 도수로 발효되어
기쁨과 슬픔의 병마개를 딸 수 있도록
언제나 병마개를 따지 않은 채
내 곁을 지키고 있는 그대여

The unopened bottle

Not an empty bottle,
But one that has yet to be unopened,

Whether filled with sorrow or overflowing with joy,
If the bottle, like a friend or lover,
Approaches, allowing me to open it together,
The presence flows through my body,
In moments of sadness and happiness alike,
It could become a lively breathing bottle for me.

The enzyme of presence,
Fermented at the right intensity,
And for me to open the bottles of joy and sorrow,
Oh, you who guard me by my side,
Always keep company without opening.

흙의 날

흙의 날을 맞아
흙으로 돌아갈 내 몸을 깨끗이 씻는다

지구를 오염시키지 않기 위해
흙으로 돌아갈
내 마음을 깨끗이 씻는다

오수를 걸러내고 있는 흙이 되어
맑은 실개천이 흐를 수 있도록
내 머릿속의 탐욕들을 정수하듯이
깨끗이 씻는다

사는 동안 내려놓지 못했던 미움들과
목숨 같았던 사랑이
한 줌의 기름진 흙이 되어
향기 그윽한 꽃 한 송이 피울 수 있도록
흙의 날을 맞아
내 일생을 정토 하듯이 깨끗이 씻는다

World Soil Day

On World Soil Day,
I thoroughly cleanse my body to return to the soil.

To avoid polluting the Earth,
I cleanse my heart, destined to return to the soil.

Becoming the soil that filters and purifies wastewater,
I cleanse my inner greed,
Distilling desires in my mind
To allow pure brooklets to flow.

The resentments I couldn't let go of in my lifetime,
And the love that was as vital as breath,
Transform into a handful of rich, fertile soil
So that a fragrant flower may bloom.
On World Soil Day,
I cleanse my entire life as if filtering soil.

대파를 썰 때면

대파를 썰며 눈물을 흘리는 것은
네가 푸른 결기로 살기 위하여
얼마나 많은 매운 세상을
속을 비워나가며 견디며 살아왔는지
네 속에 진을 치고 있었던 그 매운 세상이
풍겨 나오기 때문이리라

일편단심으로 푸른 하늘을 바라보면서
매운 세상을 삭이며
속을 비워왔던 그 매운 세월들이
대파를 썰 때면
풍겨 나오기 때문이리라

When you slice green onions,

Shedding tears while slicing green onions
Is because how much of the spicy world
You've emptied and endured
To live with a determined green spirit,
And so, the spicy world that was occupying inside
Is released.

With a single-minded heart, gazing at the blue sky,
Enduring the spiciness of the world,
The spicy years you've emptied from within,
Are emanating when you slice green onions.

빈 의자

내 마음속엔 언제나 빈 의자가 놓여 있습니다

언제쯤 그 빈 의자에 기다리던 사람이 와서 앉을지
그 빈 의자에 아름다운 꽃들이 피고 지고
녹음이 우거졌다간 낙엽이 쌓이고
눈이 내려 덮였다가 녹기를 수없이 반복하는 동안
이따금씩 새들이 날아와
나 대신 그 빈 의자에 앉아 노래도 불러주고
정처 없이 불던 바람도 가끔씩 앉아
아픈 다리를 쉬었다 가며
나의 세월을 다독거려 주었건만
언제나 내 마음은 빈 의자였었기에
흰 머리칼을 날리고 있는 갈대 바람과
세월의 목청이 늙은 새들의 노래만이
지금도 서성일 뿐

언제나 내 마음속엔 빈 의자가 놓여 있습니다

Empty Chair in My Heart

In my heart, there always lies an empty chair.

I wonder when the person who awaited
Will come and take a seat there.
While beautiful flowers bloomed and withered,
Leaves grew and fell,
Then snow endlessly covered and melted
The empty chair,
Sometimes, birds came and sat on the vacant chair,
Singing songs instead of me.
The wind, once aimlessly blowing,
Might occasionally rest there,
Resting its weary legs,
Caressing my passing years.
Yet, because my heart has always been
An empty chair,
The swaying wind rustling through my white hair,
And just old voices of birds with years
Linger and wander even now.

As always, there lies an empty chair in my heart.

바닥1

바닥은 높건 낮건
나를 이 세상을 딛게 해준다

절망의 눈물 끝이 어디까지인지
희망의 부푼 설렘이 어느 높이까지인지
알 수 없을 때에도
나를 이 세상을 딛게 해주고 있는 바닥은

어디서건 바닥을 딛고서 하늘을 바라볼 때면
언제나 내 마음속을
푸른 염원으로 채워주고 있는 바닥

The Ground 1

The ground, whether high or low,
Allows me to step on this world.

Even when I am unsure where the tears of despair end
And where the swelling excitement of hope reaches,
The ground still lets me to step on this world.

Wherever I step on the ground and look at the sky,
The ground is filling my mind with a green longing,
As always.

바닥 2

높은 곳에 있건
낮은 곳에 있건
그 바닥에 취해 헤어나지 못하면
그 바닥은 헤어 나올 수 없는 수렁이 되나니

높은 곳에 있을 땐
바닥을 딛고 서 있는 높은 산들처럼
푸른 메아리를 세상 곳곳 울려주고
낮은 곳에 있을 땐
푸른 하늘을 품에 안은 강과 바다처럼
내면을 바라보는 바닥이 돼라

The Ground 2

Whether you're in a high place
Or in a low place,
If you're unable to escape from the ground you're on,
That ground becomes an inescapable mire.

When you're in a high place,
Like tall mountains standing on the ground,
Let green hope eco around the world,
And when you're in a low place,
Like rivers and seas that cradle the blue sky,
Become a ground that gazes inward.

눈물 나는 나이

길을 가다가 보도블록 틈 사이를 비집고 나와 핀
풀꽃 한 송이를 보았을 때
눈물 나는 나이가 되어보라

그 나이가 되면
아주 소소한 도움을 베풀며 살고 있는 사람을 보아도
감동이 푸른 풀잎 구르는 이슬처럼
구르게 되고

세상을 사는 의미가
청아한 새벽, 활짝 꽃잎 펼치듯이
사랑이 물오름 하리니

황혼의 인생길을 걷다가
혹 보도블록 틈 사이를 비집고 나와 핀
풀꽃 같은 사람을 만나거든
그 자리서 목숨 같은 사랑을 다 내어줄 줄 아는
나이가 되어라

Tears Welling Age

Walking down the street, if you ever happen to glimpse a single wildflower blooming through the cracks in the pavement, try to experience the age at which tears well up in your eyes.

When you reach that age, even witnessing someone leading a humble life and offering small acts of kindness can move you deeply, like dewdrops rolling off fresh green leaves.

The meaning of life might fill with love, just like opening petals widely at the pristine dawn.

As you journey through the twilight of life, if you happen to find someone like a wildflower blooming through the cracks in the pavement, be at the age where you are willing to give all your love at that moment.

무명초의 세월

하루가 지날수록
세월이 점점 영(0)에 가까워지는 걸 보니
이제 살아갈 날이 얼마 남지 않았나보다

그동안의 희로애락도 영(0)에 가까워져가는 것 같고
살아온 세월들이 점점 무명초가 되어가는 것 같다

무명초가 되면
하나님에게 돌아갈 수 있을 것 같아
그동안 세상에서 불렸던 이름들을
하나하나 지워버린다

부질없음도 내려놓을 때
무명초가 되는 세월이여

하루가 지날수록
태어나고 죽는 것이 점점 영(0)에 가까워지는 걸 보니
이제 하나님에게로 돌아갈 날이
멀지 않았나 보다

The Years of a Nameless Weed

As each day passes,
I see time gradually approaching zero,
It seems that there are not many days left to live.

The joys and sorrows of the past
Also, seem to be nearing zero,
The years lived are turning into a nameless weed.

When it becomes a nameless weed,
I feel like I can return to God,
Erasing each name I've been called in this world.

When I also lay down futility,
The years that become anonymous.

As each day passes,
The process of being born and dying approaches zero,
It seems that the day to return to God
Is not far away.

노후의 사랑

하늘과 땅을 초월하고 있는
노후의 사랑은
이 세상을 뛰어넘는
무한대의 사랑이어라

죽음을 공유하는
노후의 사랑은
죽음도 초월하는 불후의 사랑이어라

Love in Old Age

Love in old age transcends the sky and earth
Is an infinite love that extends beyond this world,

Love in old age, facing mortality hand in hand,
Is the eternal love that outlasts mortality.

이름 없는 풀꽃에게

내가 너에게 마음을 주니
너는 나에게 와서
사랑하는 풀꽃이 되었다

내가 너를 사랑으로 바라볼 때마다
너는 나에게로 와서
내가 마음으로 속삭여주는
이름이 되었다

To the Nameless Wildflower

As I gave my heart to you,
You came to me,
Becoming the beloved wildflower.

Every time I gaze upon you with love,
You came to me,
Becoming the name whispering
By my heart.

밝음과 어둠

어둠은 누울수록 땅이 되고
밝음은 일어설수록 태양이 되는데
살아온 날이 많아질수록
자꾸만 어둠 속에 눕는 날들

어둠은 누울수록 죽음이 되고
밝음은 일어설수록 생명이 되는데

늙어가면 늙어갈수록
자꾸만 어둠 속에 눕게 되는
밝음

Brightness and Darkness

Darkness becomes the ground as it settles down,
While brightness becomes the sun as it rises.
As the days lived accumulate,
There are days when one keeps lying in the darkness.

Darkness becomes death as it lies down,
While brightness becomes life as it rises,

As one ages and grows older,
Brightness becomes lying in the darkness.

너도 그렇다

생명의 씨앗이라곤 찾아볼 수 없는
황폐한 땅에서
푸른 머릴 내밀고 있는
풀 한 포기를 보았을 때
전율하던 것처럼

너도 그렇다
모래사막 같은 내 마음에
푸른 사랑의 물결이 일렁이게 하고 있는

오아시스 같은
너의 사랑

You are like that, too

In a barren land
Where the seeds of life are nowhere to be found,
When I glimpsed a single blade of grass reaching out
With its green head,
It filled me with shivers of excitement.

You are like that, too.
In my heart, barren like a desert,
The waves of your lush love cause ripples.

Your love,
An oasis in my heart.

가벼워진다는 것은

바람이 불 때마다
몸에 밴 물을 툭툭 털고 있는
빨래 건조대에 널린 빨래들이
물이 빠질 때마다
바람처럼 몸이 가벼워졌다며
몸을 가볍게 가볍게
춤을 추고 있는 것을 보면

가벼워진다는 것은
몸에 지닌 소유를 버리면 버릴수록
자유로움의 날개라는 듯이
가벼워진 빨래들이
홀가분해진 자유로움을
나래짓고 있는 빨래 건조대

Getting Lighter

Whenever the wind blows,
Water drips from the laundry,
Hanging on the clothesline, tapping itself gently.
As the water drains away,
Claiming to have grown lighter,
Just like the wind,
Lightly, oh so lightly, it dances.

Getting lighter means,
The more possessions shed from the body,
The more wings of freedom are acquired.
The laundry, now lighter,
Flutters in the breeze,
Embodying the liberated freedom,
And dancing with its wings fluttering.

묵정밭 같은 마음에

늙어갈수록 묵정밭 같은 마음에
사랑의 꽃씨를 뿌려
향내 나는 아름다운 사랑의 꽃을 피우고 있는
그대여

혹시나 사랑의 꽃이 피고 있지 않은
묵정밭 같은 마음이 없는지
마음속 깊이깊이 간직해 두었던
최후의 유언과도 같은 사랑의 꽃씨들을
묵정밭 같은 마음 곳곳에 뿌려가며
이 세상에서 가장 향내 나게 필 수 있도록
사랑의 꽃을 피우고 있는 그대여

At the Heart like the Abandoned Field

As getting older,
At the heart like the abandoned field,
You scatter the seeds of love
And cultivate the beautiful blossoms of fragrant love.
Oh, you.

You take care if, by any chance,
There is a part of the heart like an abandoned field
Where the flowers of love are not blooming.
And you scatter the seeds of love,
Preserved deep within your heart,
Akin to the final words,
Here and there, at the heart like the abandoned field
So that the flowers of love can bloom
Most fragrantly in the world.
Oh, you.

바라보는 대상이 된다는 것은
To be the object of gaze is to be

초판 1쇄 발행_2024년 4월 15일

지은이_ 박효석

옮긴이_ 안인숙

발행처_ 오송숲

표지 디자인과 사진 _ 안인숙

출판등록_ 2020년 9월 17일 제573-2020-000027호

E-mail : osongtree@naver.com

ISBN 979-11-985399-1-5 (03810)

값 13,000 원

* 잘못 인쇄된 책은 교환해 드립니다.

이 책은 저작권법에 따라 보호를 받는 저작물이므로 무단 전재와 무단 복제를 금하며, 이 책 내용의 전부 또는 일부를 사용하려면 반드시 저작권자와 오송숲의 서면 동의를 받아야 합니다.